SPEAK!

Idea-rich tips and techniques for great presentations

Bob 'Idea Man' Hooey

Author of, Speaking for Success

SPEAK to proclaim your long-term business success!

13 steps, a shaky start

The night was dark, it was raining, and the wind was howling. There were 13 steps, in a darkened outside entrance from the dimly lit parking lot, down into the basement meeting room. **How did I know?** I counted them as I went down, went back up, and then, *screwed up* my courage and went back down again.

I descended slowly, hesitantly for the second time, reached out and nervously placed my hand on the doorknob. My heart was pumping (fast ☺), my legs were a bit shaky, and my breathing was short and labored. **Was I making the right decision?** What would I find on the other side of the door? Maybe I should just turn around and go home? How would I react? Whose crazy idea was this anyway? Would they like me, help me, or reject me? *"Ok, Hooey, go for it!"*

I put a *forced* smile on my face, turned the knob, and opened the door. I stood there for a minute, took a deep breath, and stepped into Vancouver based ***Toastmasters of Today!* I made that first step that has taken me around the world sharing my message of hope.**

I still remember my first visit that Tuesday night in April 1991. I was *nervous* and shy. Now, anyone who knows me will find that hard to believe, but it was very true, back then. This was a scary moment for me. I had just come through a devastating and debilitating divorce. Frankly, I didn't feel very confident in myself or my abilities. If you're a Toastmaster, remember your first visit to your club. Perhaps, like me, you felt a little nervous or intimidated by members who could get up and seemingly speak without notes or nervousness.

I was there, reviving a dream of being a professional speaker and someday being able to stand on the big stage sharing my ideas, travelling the world, and inspiring and investing in the lives of those in the audience.

What I found at the bottom of those 13 steps was a supportive, friendly group of people who befriended me and became my champions, coaches, and cheerleaders; some of whom still play that role in my life today.

- Perhaps you have had a similar experience as you began something?
- Perhaps you are feeling a bit shaky about starting down this path to becoming a better speaker?
- Perhaps you have played a similar role in the growth of a Toastmaster member or business friend?

That **one step** into the room, following the 13 down made an amazing difference in my life and my career. ***Update 2024:*** *I have now been a professional speaker for 25 plus years and have been to 71 countries on 6 continents, so far.*

In 1998, I had the *distinct* pleasure of walking across a Palm Desert, California stage to be inducted into the Toastmasters International Hall of Fame as the 48th professional level Accredited Speaker in our rich history. Only 81, as of 2018.

In 2008, I had the *rare* privilege of keynoting the leadership luncheon at the Toastmasters International convention. As part of my introduction they played a video of me walking across that Palm Desert stage. My first words were, ***"I may have walked across that stage by myself… but I did not get there by myself!"***

- It took those first 13 steps, ***plus*** the loving, supportive investment of thousands of fellow Toastmasters, CAPS, GSF, and NSA colleagues, over many years, to help move me toward that goal.
- It took those first 13 steps to start me on the path to living my dream of travelling the world sharing ideas and challenging people to reach out and build foundations of success under their dreams.

When I received **The Spirit of CAPS** award (the highest award given in our Canadian speaking industry) at our 2011 Canadian Association of Professional Speakers convention in Toronto, I shared it with those in attendance. I emphasized that all the nice things our President Ravi Tangri, CSP mentioned in his introduction were not accomplished, *"by myself"*. **I simply had an idea, asked for help, a lot, and got it. So, can you!**

Your dream may not be to become a professional speaker. But, if you have invested in this book my guess is you have a desire to become a better, more confident speaker, right?

You can learn to speak like a PRO! What follows in these **'SPEAK'** pages are tips, creative techniques, *proven ideas*, and exercises to help you move that dream or desire into a reality. **Ideas, when acted upon, can become forces for good that can change the world.** Evocative, engaging words reinforce those ideas and add power to your presentation inspiring people to act on your ideas.

PS: An edited version of this intro chapter was featured in *Heart of a Toastmaster*.

What is your next step?

Bob 'Idea Man' Hooey
Distinguished Toastmaster
Accredited Speaker
Past District 21 Governor
Region 4 Advisor 2018-2019
2011 Spirit of CAPS recipient
Past CAPS National Director
1998 & 1999 President CAPS BC
2012 President CAPS Edmonton

"Communication from the heart reaches a heart, communication from the head misses it by inches."

Table of Contents

**I hear and I forget,
I see and I remember,
I do and I understand!**

Confucius

These wise words were written thousands of years ago and yet they ring just as true in our 21st century lives and evolving business endeavors. We best equip those we lead with *use-it-now information*, practical tools, and applicable actions. We equip them best when we facilitate them in getting their hands dirty or in actually getting up and using what we provide.

For example: *In our presentation skills training or executive speech coaching programs, the quicker we get our students or clients up speaking, the better they learn and accelerate their learning curve. Consider the hundreds of thousands of Toastmasters around the world who nervously start speaking and find that their confidence and competence increases in direct relation to how often they are in front of an audience and in how well they apply the feedback received.*

Becoming an effective presenter is **not** learned exclusively from a book or by observing others in action. It is essentially a **learn-as-you-do** project. Kind of like life! ☺

My challenge for you is to revisit what you are doing for your own learning curve, as well as those you work with. See where you can adapt it to add more hands-on experience. How can you make it more experiential to anchor the learning and enhance the skill?

Visit our website, www.SuccessPublications.ca to check out all of Bob's Business Enhancement Success Tools (BEST) and to order your copy of the full sized, Speaking for Success!

Three key ideas to 'successful' speeches

In public speaking, the cardinal rule to being truly effective is **"NEVER BE BORING!"** Wow! But how do we do this when we are nervous and under *pressure to perform*?

I've been teaching my clients and various classes that the **"three key ideas to speaking success"** are based on acquiring the knowledge you need to successfully capture their attention, to connect with your audience, and to achieve your shared objectives.

Those three key ideas to speaking success are:
KNOW your subject or topic
KNOW your audience
KNOW yourself

If you **know your subject** and are thoroughly prepared, you will be much more relaxed and effective than if you are 'winging' it.

Taking time to organize and delve into your topic will give you a sense of the depth you bring to the platform. It will also give you much more information than you will be able to deliver, which gives you back-up information for additional presentations and questions. This confidence, based on acquired knowledge, works wonders in helping to keep the "butterflies flying in formation," as we used to say in Toastmasters.

If you **know your audience**, you will be better prepared to effectively analyze their needs and select from the body of knowledge you've acquired on your topic to serve or solve those needs; to *present* something that is relevant and helpful to them.

The better you know their backgrounds, history, connections, education, gender, and their ages; the better you will be able to construct and deliver your presentation in a way that is interesting, relevant, and informative to them.

If you **know yourself**, you can draw on your own experiences and build on your own strengths in developing your own speaking style.

You can share your own ideas and 'unique' stories in a way that allows you to be most effective. Self-knowledge is a tool of effective and successful communication.

Continually ask yourself, *"If I was in the audience, why would I be interested in this point or topic?"* Then simply make sure you have a good answer for that question. Your audiences are people, just like you. The better you know yourself, the better equipped you are to effectively reach them.

By **skillfully combining your knowledge of self, your subject, and your audience,** you will effectively increase your impact. You will also expand your impact as a presenter, interviewee, or speaker.

A final note here:
Be sure to apply the **3 Ps of public speaking –
PREPARATION, PRACTICE, and PERFORMANCE!**

There is no substitute for being prepared, by practicing until you are certain that you are ready to present your material in a confident manner. Anyone who says they just get up and *fake it* is leading you down the wrong path. Prepare, practice, and polish and then, confidently walk on stage and *play* with the audience. That is what I have learned to do, and it works well for me. **The master's *only* make it look easy.** They have put in the time, (lots of it) far from the public eye, long before they are introduced… and it shows! Share your dreams, take some risks!

Prepare yourself to WIN!

"I hated every minute of training, but I said, 'Don't quit. Suffer now and live the rest of your life as a champion.'"
Muhammad Ali

Building a successful leadership, sales career, or business takes hard work and applied energy. Becoming a competent, confident speaker does, too. Success as a speaker follows a similar path. If it was that easy, everyone would be doing it. Sometimes you will reach the end of your strength or run head-on into a roadblock or wall – **stay the course** and continue.

You **can live the rest of your life as a champion.**

- A champion of your **creativity**.
- A champion of your **courage**.
- A champion of your **causes** and concerns.
- A champion of your sales team and your **clients**.
- A champion of living and sharing/speaking your **message**.
- A champion of your successful **career** path.
- A champion of your **dreams** (turning them into reality).

This is something experienced first-hand. I worked to overcome serious challenges and difficulties to prepare for the first level audition while working towards the Accredited Speaker designation. There were times I thought about throwing in the towel. When I spoke in San Diego (1995) and was not successful, I pulled myself up and worked harder for my opportunity to speak in Saint Louis (1996).

When I fell short again, I was tempted to quit. I was frustrated, disappointed in my performance, and inclined to move on; to forget my dream of becoming a professional speaker.

9

But something would not let me quit! My success team would not let me quit either. They believed in me, even when my belief wavered.

In 1998, when I walked across a Palm Desert, California stage to become the 48th person in the world to earn this coveted professional level Toastmasters International designation; I felt like a champion who had gone 15 rounds and emerged bloodied, but unbeaten. The applause and cheers of 2000 plus fellow Toastmasters still echo in my ears. It was a pinnacle point in my life as a professional speaker; the first of many.

Was it the three speeches I prepared and presented on the TI world stage that earned this professional designation? Partially! Looking back, I believe it was the hundreds of prepared presentations given in various Toastmaster clubs and in community events across the country, as well as for paying clients that built the foundations for this eventual success on the world stage.

You can succeed in whatever field you enter if you are willing to prepare. You can become a top performing professional; be the champion you were meant to be. If I can do it, so can you!

The **Indiana University Hoosiers** basketball team were proven winners. They remained undefeated throughout their 1976 season and captured the NCAA National Championship under coach **Bobby Knight**. The '60 Minutes' commentator asked him about this amazing feat and why they were so successful. He asked, *"Was it their will to succeed?"*

"The will to succeed is important," replied Knight, *"but I'll tell you what is more important –* **it's the will to prepare**. *It's the will to go out there every day, training and building those muscles and sharpening those skills."*

- Want to be a champion salesperson? – **Prepare**

- Want to be an effective leader? – **Prepare**
- Want to create a profitable and winning business? – **Prepare**
- Want to be a powerful presenter or speaker? – **Prepare**
- Want to live an effective and meaningful life? – **Prepare**

Bill Bradley (scholar, basketball star, and former US Senator) reminds us, *"When you are not practicing, remember someone somewhere is practicing; and when you meet him or her, they will win."*

Prepare, practice, and act decisively when the time is right! Prepare and make this your time to win!

An open and shut case...

Good openings make or break your presentation and help establish a connection with your audience. We learned about openings when I joined Toastmasters twenty plus years ago. **Good openings incorporate some of these elements:**

- Tend to be short, punchy, and dramatic or thought provoking.
- Can contain a startling statement, position, intrigue, or a challenging question.
- Can incorporate an appropriate and relevant quotation, story excerpts, paradoxes, good and bad experiences, or a personal story or illustration.
- Reference a shared or common experience with your audience.
- Drawn from life, based on journalized stories, reading, listening to stories, and conversations with others.
- A general or *universal* statement that ties in or relates to your subject, while acting as an attention getter to draw them into your presentation.
- Visuals, a display, or an appropriate or relevant prop or picture.

As an audience member, you have about 30 seconds to capture my attention and draw me into the subject of your presentation.

Choose your opening words carefully.

- Avoid weak or timid openings with trite questions like; "Do you ever wonder?" "How many of you have…?" *(These have been vastly overdone in my opinion)*
- Avoid an apologetic statement or excuse such as *"I wasn't ready, but…"* **Never build a case against yourself or tell me you're not prepared… let me find out for myself!** ☺ Telling me you aren't prepared says, *"I'm not important enough for you to do your homework and prepare in advance to meet my needs."* It insults the audience.
- Don't open with a joke or humorous story unless you have it down cold. It needs to be relevant to the audience and support your presentation.

Having said that, it is important to acknowledge the person who introduced you and the audience. Most of the time I see this overdone, and it weakens your opening impact. Do it briefly and move on or start your presentation and then acknowledge them. Make sure they know you are planning it this way. Save it for a bit later, after you have the audience members hooked into your presentation! That is what I do. Very much like a movie where they show a part of it and then show the titles before moving ahead to the rest of the film.

Remember to create vivid word pictures for our minds. If you don't, we tend to think or fantasize about other areas. We think about grocery lists, work undone, or even, I'm told; fantasize about *sexual* things when we are not involved mentally. I tell my students if they smile as they leave, at least I know they've had a good time. ☺ I work to *verbally paint pictures* that challenge them to think about what I'm saying and keep them actively involved in my presentation.

Similarly, **captivating closings** are critical to your success. **Effective closings also incorporate certain key elements:**

- Summarize your major speech points and the conclusion or action drawn from them.
- Bring them back to the main theme or purpose of your presentation.
- A relevant story, illustration, or quotation that re-emphasizes the major point or central theme of your presentation.

Moving upward

"the top predictor of success and upward mobility, professionally, is how much you enjoy public speaking and how effective you are at it!"

Stanford University Survey for AT&T

"As soon as you move one step up from the bottom, your effectiveness depends on your ability to reach others through the spoken or written word."

Peter Drucker - Author

"Effective speaking skills are an essential foundation for success in any endeavor. Professionally or personally, it is one of the most important skills you'll ever acquire! And it is easily acquired!"

Bob 'idea Man' Hooey
Accredited Speaker
Presentations Skills Success Coach

Ideas to 'handle' your nervousness

Here are a few easily applied ideas and techniques on how to handle and overcome your nervousness:

1. **Don't fight it!** Realize that being a *little* nervous is normal. I accept that I am nervous and allow that nervous energy to propel me to a more impactful presentation.
2. Being **mentally prepared** is a good part of winning and Speaking for Success. Being physically prepared is another aspect of the journey.
3. Do something **physical** to work out the nervous energy.
   - Take a brisk walk.
   - Don't sit with your legs or arms crossed.
   - Let your arms dangle at your sides while you're sitting waiting to speak.
   - While your arms are dangling, twirl your wrists so your fingers shake loosely. Loosen up!
   - Pretend you're wearing a heavy overcoat or jacket and feel it on your shoulders as you shrug them up and down. Again, loosen up your shoulders.
   - Waggle your jaw back and forth a few times to loosen it up. This relaxes your face and allows you to speak better and be heard.
   - Deep breathing can help, but don't hyperventilate.
   - Use the power of self-talk, say, 'Let's go!' or use some of the affirmations. I share more in our Speaking for Success available from **www.SuccessPublications.ca**

Don't be self-conscious about having a warmup routine. Champion athletes do warmups because they know it helps them prepare to do their best. It also reduces the chance of injury. Warming up allows you to be at your best in front of an audience. It also allows you to loosen up and be more relaxed. Find out what works for you and build it into your preparation routine.

Bob's Foundations for Speaking Success!

When this material is taught in person, one of the areas covered as an overview is what I call my **'Foundations for Speaking Success!'**

Investing time to make sure you have completely thought through and answered these questions is essential to your confidence and success on the platform. These ideas were gleaned from conversations with fellow professional speakers. I've added to their wisdom from my own first-hand experience. These *'foundations'* have worked for me, and **they will work for you!** The knowledge gleaned from their *wisdom* is the secret to being able to walk confidently up to the front and deliver a message that means something to your audiences.

The secret to ensuring your audience gets the best presentation possible, with the most value, blended with personal stories and teaching points, **is in the pre-preparation**. This is what you do *well* before you start crafting your presentation.

Questions, thoughtful questions like these, can be the keys that unlock the door to success in any venture. This is no less true if your desire is to be a confident, powerful speaker, who connects with their audience, and leaves them wanting more.

- **WHY** are you speaking?
- **WHO** is your audience?
- **WHEN** will you be speaking?
- **HOW** long will you be speaking?
- **WHERE** will you be speaking?
- **WHAT** tools will you use?

Visit www.SuccessPublications.ca to order Speaking for Success which goes into much more detail in all these ideas and tips.

WHAT do you want to accomplish?
Ideas on getting to know your audience

At a NSA Platform Skills Lab training session, fellow speaker **Steve Moroski** from Atlanta, GA shared insights he'd picked up on *getting to know* his audiences. I share them from my notes and memory.

Steve encouraged us to open-up a two-way flow between our audience and ourselves prior to walking on stage.

He suggested **a few ideas to increase this flow.**

- Kick-off call to organizer to make sure we know *'who'* is coming.
- Pre-program questionnaire to organizer and audience survey.
- Gap analysis to determine areas where training or additional skills might help.
- Conference call or calls with several people who are attending.
- Email from their leader telling attendees about the upcoming session and inviting them to visit his website.
- Conversations on-site *(prior to your session)*.
- Connecting and interaction during the session.

One of the keys to being effective on the platform is in knowing your audience. The above ideas are some of the ways that I can attest work well in that regard.

"Don't use words **too big** for the subject. Don't say infinitely when you mean very; otherwise, you'll have no word left when you want to talk about something really infinite."
C.S. Lewis

Mastery of the message
Using the 3 M's of Speaking Success

I still remember the first experience of being in the 'magic of the moment.' We'd truly connected – my audience and me. They were with me fully, completely. I could take them where I wanted. WOW, what an experience! It was amazing, and nearly 25 years later, I can still vividly recall being in the moment (zone) with them and how it felt. Awesome!

Yes, I have been there since, and work to go there often, but the freshness of that experience lives on in my memory. It inspires and drives me to work diligently to prepare each session, to give my best, and to be fully there for my audiences.

That is the true 'mastery of the message' – as shown in the results and reactions of those who receive and act on it!

Mastery is an attainable skill; if you care enough and are willing to pay the price and put in the effort. I have carefully observed my CAPS, NSA, and GSF colleagues and speaker friends. I have watched those who are acknowledged *master's* on the platform and in the training room, to see what they do and what they bring to their mastery. Each has their own unique style and substance. Each has a shared commitment to mastery and serving their audience's highest needs.

So, let's explore the **3 Ms of Speaking Success™** that lead to the mastery of the message and give you entrance into the magic of the shared moment.

Message

First, make sure you have something to say!

This should be a given, but it isn't to many emerging speakers. All too often, I have seen beginning speakers who simply *parrot* something they've read or heard from another speaker or author. It is not real in their lives or relevant for them or for their audiences and it shows. You need to adopt it, live it!

Not that sharing a message *gleaned* from a master or a group of master's is a bad thing. Presenting it as though it is your own is! It is unprofessional and borders on plagiarism or intellectual property theft. **DON'T DO IT!** Make sure you've *fully* researched your material, so you have some depth and are not just another 'book-report' speaker.

To reach your audience you need to *filter your message* through your life and your experiences to make sure it is real and relevant to them. If it is not real or relevant to you, it won't connect, and you'll fail.

- How well do you know your audience? What do you know about them that would guide you in the research and the crafting of your message?
- How much time have they given you to share it?
- What gems of wisdom, what stories, what experiences can you draw on to flesh it out and make your message live, connect, and remain embedded in their hearts?
- What do you want them to learn, understand, or act on from your message?

Dig deep in your message and prepare well in advance.

The master's never shirk their diligence in preparation!

Messenger

You as the messenger bear a strong responsibility for the success of your message being received and acted upon by your audiences.

It needs to be fully integrated and involved in your life to become real and relevant to them. It needs to be in line with what you truly believe to be credible and, even more importantly, achievable by action on their part.

They will believe your message and act on it when they believe you!

What is your motive and motivation for speaking to them? It is important to know 'why' you are speaking and where you are coming from, if you would seek to succeed with them, connect with them, and impact their lives.

Be honest with yourself in what you seek here. Do you seek to simply entertain yourself at their expense, use them for therapy? Or are you seeking to impart and inspire them to gain knowledge, take action, and rally around the flag to a better life or a more effective career or business?

The masters know themselves and share openly and boldly!

Knowing yourself helps you take what you know about them and apply it in crafting your message and in more skillfully delivering it.

Method

This is the *easier* part of the presentation equation. ☺ If you've dug deep enough to make sure what you have to say is truly valuable and has relevance to your audience, make sure it is in-line with your own integrity and life; it will be so much easier to communicate effectively to an audience.

Once you've decided what outcome you desire from the communication of your message, it is easier to structure the delivery system. Depending on the message and the desired outcome, (*and of course the time constraints of the time you must deliver it*), you can blend in stories, audience interaction and exercises, and inspirational bits.

Time is one of the biggest factors that impact the delivery method you choose.

I've grown to love the interaction with audiences. I find when keynoting, that my ability to incorporate active dialogue with them is more challenging than during breakouts and training sessions. That being said, I still work in some areas where they can actively give feedback or respond to the message being shared.

Asking questions, getting them to share something with a neighbor, or simply using rhetorical questions to draw them in; all these techniques will work in building a bridge to the hearts and minds of your audiences.

The effective use of storytelling is *under-rated* and ignored by speakers in many levels and arenas. Sometimes the most effective way to communicate a message is to wrap it tenderly in a story. How many Sunday school lessons do you still remember; how many nursery rhymes or children's stories can you still recall? My bet, lots of them – and if you can recall the story, you can retain the lesson and the message behind the story.

The masters weave stories to last a lifetime!

A few final ideas...

If you want to achieve the 'mastery of the message' you will need to dig deep to master yourself first and then draw from that in preparing and delivering your message. **Applying the 3 M's will help you succeed.**

You owe it to your audiences to diligently prepare and to bring forth your best. Anything else would be a waste of everyone's time and energy.

Seeking to become a '*master of the message*' is the beginning of attaining the mastery – and the journey is worth it!

Use story starters to warm up your brain.

To get you started, I've included a few of my own story starters. These story starters give my brain a mental kick and get me thinking about something I might put into an easy format to capture and share an idea. Perhaps they will work for you too?

Ideas on using a 'How to' story starter:

- How I learned the importance of _____.
- How I got started in the _____ business.
- My worse Customer Service experience: why? _____.
- My favorite customer: why? _____.
- The best lesson I learned last year_____.
- Something funny happened to me: _____.
- How to overcome _____.
- How to initiate _____.
- How to unravel the secret of _____.
- My dream company: _____why?
- The best lesson I've learned here at _____.

"Write to be understood, speak to be heard, read to grow." **Lawrence Clark Powell**

Class notes and ideas

This section draws from slides and ideas used in my various on-site or live classes. I expound and expand on elements from each one, based on my own experience and application. On site, I spend time sharing my own stories and on-stage lessons to help my students grasp and built on these ideas. This made this course a favorite at several colleges in the Vancouver area for the 6 or so years where I taught. In fact, one college voted me the 'most marketable instructor' and gave me a nice plaque. Their sales staff often used my series of presentation skills classes as a selling or closing point when enrolling new students. Being they were on commission, I found this very interesting.☺

I've drawn these **'class notes'** from many sources: books I've studied, notes taken, in depth conversations, observations, and Q&A sessions with fellow professionals, my Toastmasters experience, and my own experiences on the platform over nearly 25 years.

Make a point of personalizing or internalizing them to your own specific situation and needs. Use the ones that apply to the type of presentation and style you've chosen.

Touching on the basics

Speaker Dorothy Leeds, best-selling author of '**POWER SPEAK**' has built a very successful career working with people by helping them be more effective as presenters. Dorothy discovered that most of her clients and struggling speakers had a pattern of flaws leading to ineffective speaking.

These **six major faults** in speaking often separate the *successful* speaker from the *mediocre* speaker. *In our live classes this section is prefaced with a story of growing up in California and living close to a fault line; a fault line that made the ground less stable and more susceptible to earthquakes.* When you craft your presentation make sure you build on solid foundations.

Give some thought to each of the six speaking faults. Have you seen it in your own presentations? Have you seen it in the efforts of others?

How would you avoid each fault or minimize it in your own speaking?

- **An unclear purpose** *(direction)*
- **Lack of clear organization and leadership** *(structure)*
- **Too much information or data** *(content)*
- **Not enough support for your ideas, concepts, or information** *(research)*
- **Monotonous voice or sloppy speech habits** *(speaking style)*
- **Not meeting the real needs of the audience** *(research)*

Keep in mind, challenging each of these speaking 'faults' face-on is an opportunity to grow as a speaker. There is not one fault listed here that cannot be overcome or minimized in your striving to be a better speaker.

'Miracles' occur when students/clients apply their efforts and focus to replacing these faults with strong foundations; and in practicing until those foundations are strong enough to support them effectively. **You can too!**

Platform professional **Ira M. Hayes** shared several focus points he considered necessary to successful presentations. I adapted his ideas and frequently share these with my students as the '**SEVEN BE-ATTITUDES**' of Effective Speaking.

1. **BE -** informative
2. **BE -** valuable
3. **BE -** interesting
4. **BE -** memorable
5. **BE -** believable

6. Strive to **BE -** inspirational
7. **BE -** enjoyable!

Give some thought on how to best incorporate these **BE-attitudes** into your presentations. When you apply some new attitudes, you often get some new responses from your audiences.

Speaking professional **Ty Boyd,** CSP, CPAE, from Charlotte, NC had **ten points or building blocks for success** he felt you needed to be effective as a communicator. Based on his long and successful run as a professional speaker, I took note! His lessons live on in those of us who apply them in our careers. When he spoke at NSA in Orlando, at 80 years old, he still had it! He still brought it! I was inspired…Thanks Ty!

1. **FIRE** in your belly
2. Have **FOCUS**
3. Good speakers **PERFORM**
4. Use **COLOR** in your voice, your body, and your energy
5. Use your face – **SMILE!**
6. Use the rest of your **BODY** too (be aware of body language)
7. Learn to effectively use your **EYES**
8. Maintain physical **BALANCE**
9. **INVOLVE** your audience
10. **PRACTICE, practice, practice!**

One of the biggest *misconceptions* of public speaking I've encountered over the years is people's persistence in separating platform style presentations from one-to-one meeting or smaller group presentations.

Often this is simply a matter of perception, **"Oh my, I have to give a presentation!"** People in business – powerful people – have learned to harness the power of speaking whenever and wherever they are communicating verbally.

You can too, using some of the tips and techniques outlined in this little guidebook.

One question I frequently get from my clients and students is **"How do you give your presentations without notes?"** A good question! Sometimes I do use notes. I don't have a problem with having someone using them, as long as they are unobtrusive and don't take audience focus away from your presentation. There are several famous speakers who effectively use notes in their presentations.

Using notes as a back-up to give you a sense of confidence is okay. So is using notes as reference or to quote a fact or quotation. Keep them simple and don't get in the habit of depending on them or obviously referring to them during your presentation.

One exercise shared with my students was to ask them to hold up and look at their hand. **"What do you see?"** They usually say, **"A thumb and four fingers,"** which is of course, the obvious answer.

My answer to that same question is **"A presentation, without notes, up to 20 minutes."** I see an opening, three points and a conclusion.

I can remember 5 points or 5 things! Can't you? When we keep it simple and focus on the main points it makes it easier to remember.

Using gestures

Here are a few ideas on using gestures to add movement and energy to your presentation. Effective use of gestures enhances your audience connection.

- **Use gestures** to channel your nervous muscle tension by carefully selecting or choreographing body movements that emphasize specific speech points. Nervous energy can effectively be used to lend welcome animation to your movements and presentation.
- Using **gestures** effectively is a whole area of its own, but a few points must be made here. Audiences will believe what they see in your face, manners and body movement long BEFORE they believe what you say.

Gestures can amplify your speech by including facial expressions and body language to illustrate pain, pleasure, sarcasm, sincerity, enthusiasm, or disinterest, as well as other emotions.

Here are a few more story starters for you.
Use them to kick start your brain or perhaps as the basis for a story to include in one of your speeches.

Ideas for your use as a foundation for a story:

- The number 1 principle for success _____:
- 2 ways of approaching _____:
- 3 questions to ask when _____:
- 4 cornerstones of _____:
- 5 key elements of _____:
- 6 steps to creating a _____:
- 7 ways to _____:
- 8 secrets of _____:
- 9 lies or myths in the _____:
- 10 tips when using _____:

"When the trust account is high, communication is easy, instant, and effective." **Stephen R. Covey**

Five Steps to persuasion
...ideas to create successful presentations

In essence, every presentation aims to persuade an audience. We seek to persuade them to listen and perhaps agree with what we present. Crafting our thoughts and ideas, with this in mind, is what proves our professionalism.

- **Get their attention:** If you don't capture my attention, you'll never gain my acceptance or my action on your behalf. What does it take to do that? Do it!
- **Demonstrate their need to know:** This is where you help me see the relevance of what you are about to share. If I don't see a need in my life, career, or company I will not respond favorably to your call to action and you are wasting both of our time.
- **Satisfy that need:** This is where you outline the solutions in ways that I can apply and benefit.
- **Visualize the results:** Help me see the *finished* results; the changes as outlined in your solution. Give me a *mental* picture of my need being met and my satisfaction attained, and I will be more receptive to act or buy.
- **Request their action:** This is where many mediocre salespeople blow it. **Ask for the order**. Call me to action! Challenge me to do something great!

This is a summary of the steps behind persuasion. Keep them in mind as you structure your presentation. Keep in mind what the audience reaction will be to each area. Selling your ideas as a presenter is very similar to what profession salespeople do with their clients and the process follows a similar path.

"People will pay a dollar for a program with information, but they'll pay $ 10 for a program with information plus a story."
Brian Tracy

Using humor... a few safety tips

In the professional speakers' world there is a saying in response to the question, **"Do you have to be funny?"** (Pause) **"Only, if you want to be paid!"**

While that is not entirely true, humor, when properly used, does make your presentation more interesting and helps build bridges with your audience.

Here are a few tips to remember if you plan on including relevant humor:

- Punch lines? Remember them!!!! Practice until you can nail it if awoken from a dead sleep.
- Ensure the anecdote/story is appropriate and relates to your presentation – not just inserted for the laughs. Too many amateurs undermine their efforts when they insert something funny that doesn't relate to their audiences.
- Timing is everything – practice it! A lot!!!
- BE KIND! Don't pick on any group or person. Pick on yourself! This also helps build bridges with your audience by showing you are a real person.
- Vulgarity and sexist remarks are NOT allowed. They always work against you.
- Humor doesn't travel well. Make sure it works in different locations. Humor doesn't always translate to other cultures.

While speaking in Tehran, Iran (2009) I shared a story that always got a laugh in North America. Nothing! No laughter, no chuckles, nothing. I asked the translator about it, and he said, "I didn't get it!" Once I explained it to him, he laughed. He got it.

Later that week we used it again in Kish to 300 university students; and we got laughs, lots of laughs. He helped me bridge the cultural laughter wall.

Presentation tip

Why would you want to take the extra time and effort it takes to make an effective presentation? What would it accomplish?

What is your motivation for investing your time in researching, creating, or crafting and then practicing and honing it before you deliver it?

An effective presentation:

- Demonstrates that you are thoroughly **prepared** and have done your homework.
- Has its information well **organized** in a complete, logical, and concise format.
- Reveals your human side and acts as a **catalyst** to connect with your audience.
- Reveals your **competency** – demonstrates that you do indeed have the skill set and the ability to successful complete your assignment or project.
- Consistently **keeps your audience** awake and aware of your actions.

"If you are not born with gifted skills of powerful communication, influence, or elite level performance naturally, fear not. This is a learnable skill, and one you can learn to simply engage everyone who experiences you or take it to the world stage and become someone in a position of significance, power and authority."
Mark Eriksson

Speaking for Success, available from www.successpublications.ca is a great resource if this is an area where you want to grow and excel.

Copyright and license notes

SPEAK! *Idea-rich tips and techniques for great presentations*

Bob 'Idea Man' Hooey, Accredited Speaker, 2011 Spirit of CAPS recipient. Prolific author of 30 plus business, leadership, and career success publications

Photos of Bob: **Dov Friedman**, www.photographybyDov.com
Bonnie-Jean McAllister, www.elantraphotography.com
Editorial, layout and design: **Irene Gaudet,** Vitrak Creative Services, vitrakcreative.com

ISBN: 9781998014095

Printed in the United States 10 9 8 7 6 5 4 3 2 1
Success Publications – a division of Creativity Corner Inc.
Box 10, Egremont, AB T0A 0Z0
www.successpublications.ca
Creative office: 1-780-736-0009

"An idea is a feat of association." **Robert Frost**

Acknowledgements, credits, and disclaimers

תודה
Dankie Gracias
Спасибо Merci شكرا Takk
Köszönjük Terima kasih
Grazie Dziękujemy Děkujame
Ďakujeme Vielen Dank Paldies
Kiitos Täname teid 謝謝

Thank You Tak

感謝您 Obrigado Teşekkür Ederiz
Σας Ευχαριστούμ 감사합니다
Bedankt Děkujeme vám ขอบคุณ
ありがとうございます
Tack

As with each of my books, a very special dedication of this piece of myself, to the two people who meant the most to me, my folks **Ron and Marge Hooey**. Sadly, both my parents left this earthly realm in 1999. I still miss our time together and your encouragement and love. I was blessed with the two of you in my life. I've added **George and Lillian Sidor** (Irene's folks) to this gratitude list.

To my inspiring wife and professional proofreader and publications coach, **Irene Gaudet**, who loves, encourages, and supports me in my quest to continue sharing my **Ideas At Work!** across the world. Thank you seems so inadequate for your timely work in helping make my writing and my client service better! I love the time we spend together!

To my **colleagues and friends** in Toastmasters, the National Speakers Association (NSA), the Canadian Association of Professional Speakers (CAPS), and the Global Speakers Federation (GSF) who continually challenge me to strive for success and increased excellence.

To my **great audiences, leaders, students, coaching clients, and readers** across the globe who share their experiences and enjoyment of my work. Your positive and supportive feedback encourages me to keep working on additional programs and success publications like this updated version. My experience with you creates the foundation for additional real-life experiences I can take from the stage to the page, the classroom to the boardroom.

My thanks to a select few friends for your ongoing support and 'constructive' abuse. You know who you are. ☺

Disclaimer

We have not attempted to cite all the authorities and sources consulted in the preparation of this book. To do so would require much more space than is available. The list would include departments of various governments, libraries, industrial institutions, periodicals, and many individuals. Inspiration was drawn from many sources, including other books by the author; in this updated creation of this min-version of 'SPEAK!'

'Speak!" is written and designed to provide information on more creative use of your time, as a business leader's enhancement guide. It is sold with the 'explicit' understanding that the publisher and/or the author are not engaged in rendering legal, accounting, or other Professional services. If legal or other expert assistance is required, the services of a competent Professional in your geographic area should be sought.

It is not the purpose of this mini book to reprint all the information that is otherwise available. Its primary purpose is to complement, amplify, and supplement other books and reference materials already available. You are encouraged to search out and study all the available material, learn as much as possible, and tailor the information to your individual needs. This will help to enhance your success in being a more effective salesperson, leader or professional.

Every effort has been made to make this book as complete and as accurate as possible within the scope of its focus. However, there may be mistakes, both typographical and in content or attribution. Graphics are royalty free or under license. Care has been taken to trace ownership of copyright material contained in this volume. The publisher will gladly receive information that will allow him to rectify any reference or credit line in subsequent editions. This book should be used only as a general guide and not as the ultimate source of information. Furthermore, this book contains information that is current only up to the date of publication.

The purpose of 'SPEAK!' is to educate and entertain; perhaps to inform and to inspire. It is certainly to challenge its readers to learn and apply its secrets and tips, to challenge them to enhance their skills and leverage their efforts to create more Productive outcomes. The author and publisher shall have neither liability nor responsibility to any person or entity with respect to any loss or damage caused, or alleged to have been caused, directly or indirectly, by the information contained in this book.

Bob's B.E.S.T. publications

Bob is a *prolific* author who has been capturing and sharing his wisdom and experience in print and electronic formats for the past fifteen plus years. In addition to the following publications, several of them best sellers, he has written for consumer, corporate, trade, professional associations, and on-line publications. He has been engaged to write and assist on publications by other best-selling writers and successful companies.

Bob's **B**usiness **E**nhancement **S**uccess **T**ools

Leadership, business, and career success series
Running TOO Fast (8th edition 2022)
Legacy of Leadership (5th edition 2024)
Make ME Feel Special! (6th edition 2022)
Why Didn't I 'THINK' of That? (5th edition 2022)
Speaking for Success! (10th edition 2023)
THINK Beyond the First Sale (3rd edition 2022)
Prepare Yourself to WIN! (3rd edition 2018)

Bob's mini-book success series
The Courage to Lead! (4th edition 2024)
Creative Conflict (3rd edition 2024)
Get to YES! (5th edition 2023)
THINK Before You Ink! (3rd edition 2017)
Running to Win! (2nd edition 2024)
Generate More Sales (5th edition 2023)
Unleash your Business Potential (3rd edition 2023)

Learn to Listen (2nd edition 2017)
Creativity Counts! (3rd edition 2016)
Create Your Future! (3rd edition 2024)

Bob's Pocket Wisdom series *(coming as e-books in 2024)*
Pocket Wisdom for **Selling Professionals**
Pocket Wisdom for **Speakers** (updated 2023)
Pocket Wisdom for **Innovators**
Pocket Wisdom for **Leaders – Power of One!** (updated 2023)
Pocket Wisdom for **Business Builders**

Co-authored books created by Bob
Quantum Success – 3 volume series (2006)
In the Company of Leaders (3rd edition 2014)
Foundational Success (2nd edition 2013)

Bob's Idea-rich leaders edge series (new 2018-2023)
LEAD! *12 idea-rich leadership success strategies*
CREATE! *Idea-rich strategies for enhanced innovation*
TIME! *Idea-rich tips for enhanced performance and productivity*
SERVE! *Idea-rich strategies for enhanced customer service*
SPEAK! *Idea-rich tips and techniques for great presentations*
CREATIVE CONFLICT *Idea-rich leadership for team success*

Visit: www.SuccessPublications.ca for more information on
Bob's publications and other success resources.

Email: bob@ideaman.net or visit:
www.SuccessPublications.ca

"Innovation is a learned skill of
observation and application
– Ideas At Work!"
Bob 'Idea Man' Hooey
'My 'NEXT' Million Dollar Idea Book'

What they say about Bob 'Idea Man' Hooey

I frequently travel across North America, and more recently around the globe, sharing my **Ideas At Work!**

I am fortunate to get feedback and comments from my audiences and colleagues. These comments come from people who have been touched, challenged, or simply enjoyed themselves in one of my sessions.

"I still get comments from people about your presentation. Only a few speakers have left an impression that lasts that long. You hit a spot with the tourism people." **Janet Bell**, Yukon Economic Forums

"Thank you, Bob, *it is always a pleasure to see a true professional at work. You have made the name 'Speaker' stand out as a truism - someone who encourages people to examine their lives and adjust. The comments indicated you hit people right where it is important - in their hearts. Each of those in your audience took away a new feeling of personal success and encouragement."* **Sherry Knight**, Dimension Eleven Human Resources and Communications

*"I am pleased to recommend **Bob 'Idea Man' Hooey** to any organization looking for a charismatic, confident speaker and seminar leader. I have seen Bob in action on several occasions, and he is ALWAYS on! Bob has the ability to grab his audience's attention and keep it. Quite simply, if Bob is involved - your program or seminar is guaranteed to succeed."* **Maurice Laving**, Coordinator Training and Development, London Drugs

"On very short notice Bob cleared his schedule and graciously presented at our meeting when the original Speaker was unable to attend. **Last week Bob set the tone for our two-day leadership meeting and gave us all a motivational lift.** *His compassion and true interest in people was clearly evident, making him very credible. He shared some great stories, has a wealth of experience and knowledge and it was a pleasure listening to him. His down-to-Earth style makes it easier to retain the information presented. He also followed up with additional info and handouts, cementing his message of building bridges, not walls. Fantastic job, Bob, and thanks again!"* **Barbara Afra Beler**, MBA, Senior Specialist Commercial Community, Alberta North, **BMO Bank of Montreal**

*"I have been so excited working with Bob Hooey, as he has given inspiration and motivation to our leadership team members. Both at the Brick Warehouse – Alberta and here at Art Van Furniture – Michigan; with his years of experience in working with business executives and his humorous and delightful packaging of his material, he makes **learning with Bob a real joy**. But most importantly, anyone who encounters his material is the better for it."*
Kim Yost, CEO Art Van Furniture, former CEO The Brick

Motivate your teams, your employees, and your leaders to 'productively' grow and 'profitably' succeed!

Protect your conference investment - leverage your training dollars.

Enhance your professional career and sell more products and services.

Equip and motivate your leaders and their teams to grow and succeed, 'even' in tough times!

Leverage your time to enhance your skills, equip your teams, and better serve your clients.

Leverage your leadership and investment of time to leave a significant legacy!

Call today to engage best-selling author, award winning, inspirational leadership keynote speaker, leaders' success coach, and employee development trainer, **Bob 'Idea Man' Hooey** and his innovative, audience based, results-focused, **Ideas At Work!** for your next company, convention, leadership, staff, training, or association event. You'll be glad you did!

Call 1-780-736-0009 to connect with Bob 'Idea Man' Hooey today!

Learn more about Bob at:
www.ideaman.net or
www.BobHooey.training

37

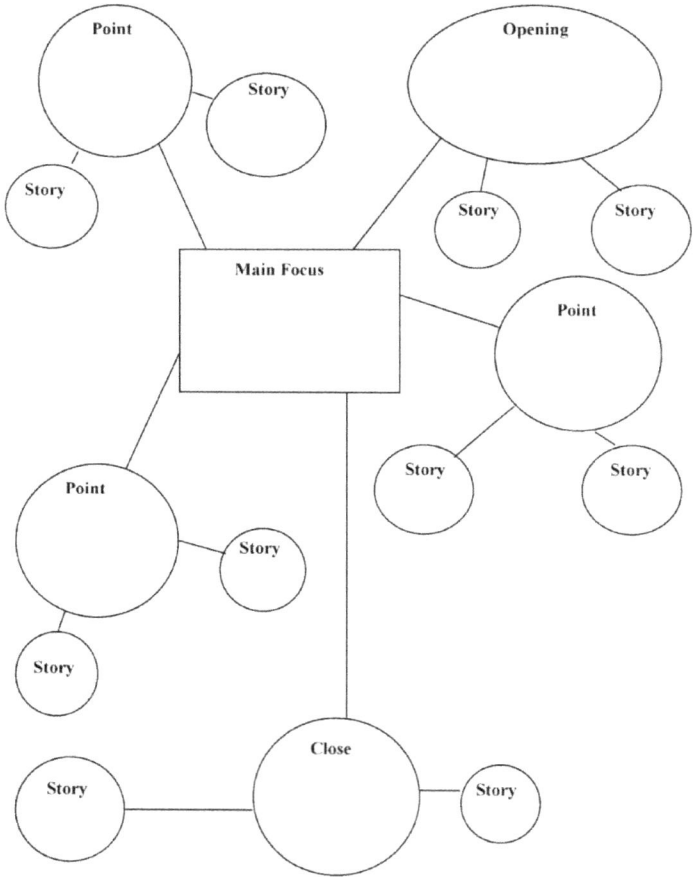

Sample Speech Outline

This is a stylized example of mind mapping that I use when creating a presentation. Simply, note the main ideas, connect the examples or stories to support it and then, decide on how to order them as you speak.

More information on this and other ideas in Speaking for Success available from www.SuccessPublications.ca